How To Raise Your Credit Score

The Ultimate Guide To Your Total Money Makeover: Tips and Strategies- For Saving Money, Credit Repair, and Becoming Debt Free

Introduction

Hello, I want to thank you and congratulate you for downloading the book, *The Ultimate Guide to Your Total Money Makeover: Tips and Strategies-For Saving Money, Credit Repair, and Becoming Debt Free*.

This book contains proven steps and strategies on how to save money and get yourself in better financial shape.

In this book we're going to talk about three different aspects of financial success. We're going to explain how you can and should go about saving more money and what you need to do in order to make sure that you eliminate debt.

Getting yourself in the best possible financial shape is important to your overall success in life. After all, without the right amount of money to support yourself and your family it's nearly impossible to do everything that you want and that's what life is all about right? You want to be able to enjoy yourself as much as possible.

But in order to truly live a happy life you need to make sure that you are financially stable and that means saving money, getting your credit in good shape and eliminating debt.

Thanks again for downloading this book, I hope you enjoy it!

Chapter 1: Budgeting Your Money, The Easy Way

If you're looking to get out of debt the most important thing you need to do is make sure you know where your money is going. You want to make sure that you understand how much you owe to each place, company or person and then you'll be able to take the time and make the effort to actually create a budget that works.

For many people, the very idea of creating a budget is daunting. How can you possibly figure out how much money you should send to everyone when you don't even really know how much money you have or how much money you owe or which one you should pay off first? There's just too many questions involved and you find yourself completely thrown off and confused.

That's why step one is making sure you know how much you owe and to whom. Start by making a list of all the information you have. List the amount of money that's owed, who you owe it to and whether the amount is currently a collection or is just 'past due.' Both of these categories are important but knowing the difference will help you understand which to pay off first.

Past due accounts are those that you owe to a credit company but they are still contacting you asking for payment. They haven't revoked your credit yet, they're just tacking on a lot of fines, fees and interest for as long as you don't pay the account. These accounts are going to look back on your credit report (which we'll talk about later) but they aren't going to be as bad as collection accounts. These types of accounts are generally capable of being paid off in monthly payments (regular credit card payments)

A collection account is one where the credit company has completely given up on getting their money back. What they do is they sell the debt to a collection agencies and that agency attempts to get the money back from you. This is money that has been overdue for a long period of time and you know owe the entire amount is due all at the same time. In some instances you can get the company to take payments or accept a lower settlement but you're generally responsible for the entire account.

When you're working on creating a budget you want to make sure you're paying at least a little bit of money on each of your past due accounts because this encourages them to keep the account open. They want to get as much money from you as possible and if they choose to close the account and turn it into a collection that won't happen. So they keep the account open as long as you continue to pay (even if you aren't making full monthly payments and the fees are still racking up.

With a collection you need to contact the company if you want to attempt to make payments (usually not easy) or you need to pay off the entire amount (or settlement amount) all at the same time. This means you need to come up with all the money or you really can't do anything about the account.

When you create your budget you want to think about everything that you have coming into the home and then think about every bill that you have. The bills that are considered current you want to keep current. These are helping your credit score even as other past due bills are hurting it. These are bills like your lights, electricity, water and food. Make sure you have enough money set aside monthly to pay for all of these things. Determine how much money you need in order to pay off those current bills and then look at what's left over. A portion of this should go into a savings account. Try to get at least $50 to go to savings every month. This will help you slowly build up a little nest egg in case of emergencies.

The money that's left over needs to be divided over the rest of your past due bills. Try to at least reach the minimum payment amount on your credit cards or accounts that are considered past due. This will help you keep from getting additional fees for not meeting the minimum payment amount. If you can afford to pay the amount that's past due you'll be even better off but try to keep the account open. That means you want to keep some type of charge on the account so they don't close it.

If you're past due on an account it's more likely that they will close the account once they get your money. As we'll talk about in a later chapter, this isn't something that you want to happen. That means you want to keep a balance on the card but try to keep it current instead of past due. This will help you build your credit back up.

Once you've taken the minimum payment amount for each of your past due accounts try to see what's left. If there's anything left see if it will come close to the payoff amount for one of your collection accounts. If it's close you may be able to negotiate with the company (which we'll discuss in our chapter about collection agencies).

Your budget should go somewhere that you can see it easily and often. You don't want to mess up your budget because that's going to keep you on track with your spending and with paying off bills. That will get you out of debt faster and help you get back to having fun with your money (instead of giving it to everyone else for nothing).

Chapter 2: Dispute the Charges

You should always keep an eye on your credit report. There are plenty of credit card companies and even websites that will provide it to you completely free so make sure you're taking advantage of that feature. You'll be able to monitor if someone ever steals your identity and you're also going to be able to keep track of the accounts that are affecting your credit score both in positive and negative ways.

If you look at your credit report and see a lot of negative accounts, such as past due or collection accounts, consider whether they are accurate. Did you know that the credit reporting agencies are required by law to ensure that your credit report is 100% accurate at all times? If it's not they are required (also by law) to remove the incorrect information.

What this means to you is that, if the negative accounts on your credit report are not 100% accurate you can request to have them removed. What you want to do is review your report and consider which accounts may not be correct. Now keep in mind you're not allowed to dispute anything that is true. So if the negative account on your credit report is accurate you're supposed to leave it alone. If it's not, write a letter to the credit reporting agency (that's Transunion, Equifax or Experian) and ask them to remove it. Let them know why it needs to be removed and make sure you include your name, birthdate and social security number in the letter.

If you do this then the credit reporting agency is required to investigate and make sure the account is accurate. If it is then they will send you a letter verifying the account and request that if you have evidence that it's not accurate you send that information to them. If it is not accurate they must remove it from your credit report and your credit score will be updated to reflect it.

Writing letters to the credit reporting agencies doesn't always work 100%. Sometimes they will continue to tell you an account has been verified when you know it isn't accurate. If this happens you'll have to go above their heads and write to the original creditor, letting them know that the account is inaccurate and providing information that verifies this. This could be statements showing your bills were paid on time or letters indicating that they removed the account. Remember to send copies of these documents and not the actual letter.

Disputing false information can get a lot of accounts dropped and it can remove some of your debt because you won't have to pay for those collections or past due charges if you can prove that they are not accurate. Plus this is going to improve your credit score and repair your credit because the negative accounts are being removed.

Chapter 3: Negotiate With Credit Companies

Another thing not a lot of people know is that you can negotiate with credit companies. So you're able to take the collection letter they send you or a past due notice that has been sent to you and discuss it with them. In many cases they will take a lower amount than what's on the bill just so that they can guarantee they'll get something

Let's say you owe Discover $1,000. They really want to get their money so they send you a past due notice. But for several months you've ignored that past due notice and now they've sent it to collections. The collections agency may offer you a settlement. Maybe they say they'll take $900 if you just pay it to them right then and there. You have the opportunity to call them and request that they take a lesser amount.

If you talk to the collection agency and they agree to take a lesser amount you will have to send that payment in full. Make sure that when you send them the check you write out the words 'paid in full' on the check. Make a copy of the check for your own records as well. Once they cash that check your account is legally considered to be paid in full and they are no longer able to come after you for more money.

In many cases an original creditor or a collection agency will accept less than the bill is for just because they want to get something. They know that if you've ignored them for this long you may continue to do so and they may never be able to get any money out of you. In fact, a large number of people who have immense debts and a lot of collections out for them will just go bankrupt and then those companies never get anything. That's why they are willing to accept lower payments. A lower payment will guarantee them something for their trouble and it will allow them to close out the account.

Chapter 4: Cut the Credit Cards

If you're looking to save some money then you need to make sure you're spending less. That means getting rid of all those credit cards. If you have a lot of credit cards you're going to be tempted to use them and that's not going to help you save anything. So what you want to do is get rid of the credit cards.

One thing it's important to remember is that actually closing out your credit cards is probably going to decrease your credit score. When you have less available credit (the amount of money that the credit card companies allow you to spend) your amount of credit used increases. What you want to do is make sure that you keep a few credit cards so you have a decent amount of available credit. You want to avoid using them however.

If you're able to avoid the temptation to purchase things you can put one credit card in the back of your purse or wallet. Choose a card that will work anywhere such as a major credit card company. This is for emergencies only. An emergency doesn't mean you found something that you really want to have. It means that your car broke down and needs to be towed, or you run out of gas.

The rest of the credit cards you decide to keep should be locked up somewhere in your home. Put them in a safe or lockbox. This way you have to actively think about getting the card out again before you're able to actually use it. This will keep you from using the card in a spur of the moment fashion and will ensure that you still have it available if absolutely necessary.

Stop using credit cards as much as possible. This will allow you to save more money because you won't have to spend a lot of your money on credit card bills at the end of the month. Instead, you'll have all the money you would have spent on those bills left over to put in a savings account. Remember that budget you made at the beginning of this book and make sure that you stick to it. Don't spend too much of your money on things you don't need throughout the month.

Keep in mind that if you don't use your credit card at all it's eventually going to be taken away from you. That's because the credit card companies don't want to allow credit to someone that isn't going to do anything with it and eventually they will cancel your account. This is going to lower the amount of available credit you have and it's going to decrease your credit score.

The best thing to do is make one to two small purchases on your credit card every few months. Try to space out using different cards so that none of them get taken but you don't owe very much money each month. You want to keep the amount negligible. That means it's low enough that it really doesn't affect your overall budget. This is going to let you keep the card but, at the same time, it's not going to completely break the bank.

Chapter 5: Understanding Your Credit Report

Your credit report is not all that easy to understand. There are a lot of different categories in the report and that means you need to weigh out different things in order to make sure that your credit score is going to be high enough for you to get the things you want.

The best scores are those that are over 900 but not many people are actually able to achieve that. If your score is over a 700 you actually have really good credit and you're pretty much guaranteed any type of credit that you might apply for. But you want to keep in mind that different types of credit card companies or credit agencies will want a different score.

If your score is in the 600's you have a decent chance of getting credit in most places but not all. This isn't guaranteed however. There are plenty of agencies that will consider you a little bit of a risk.

Your credit score is actually an indication of how much of a risk it is to give you credit.

When you first start out getting credit you have a low credit score. This tells the person checking your score that there is a high level of risk involved. They don't know if you're going to pay the bills or if you're going to rack up high amounts of charges. That's why your score is low. As you get more recorded payments your score will go up because the risk of you not paying for things is getting lower.

Now it's not just late payments or missed payments that are going to count against you in regards to your credit score. There are actually a lot of different factors that cause problems with your credit score (or improve your credit score)

So let's break them down a little and look at what's on your credit report.

Public records are one of the first things that show up on your credit report. These are the worst things you can have, judgments and tax liens against you. Any of these are going to make a big dent in your credit score and they're going to continue to work against you for a very long time (up to 7 years). You definitely don't want these if you can help it.

The next thing is going to be your credit items. These are credit cards, loans, mortgages and any other credit account that you've had in the past. Most accounts that are considered old (closed more than 10 years ago) will not report unless you've had a collection filed for that account.

Each of your credit items is going to count towards your credit score. Every on time payment is going to count in your favor and every late payment, missed payment or collection is going to count against you. Each balance is going to be reported as well and high balances are also going to count against you.

Remember we said before that you want to have a high available credit balance but you also want to have a low balance on the credit you're using. What the credit reporting agency does is look at how much you're able to spend on all of your credit cards and add that together. That's your available credit balance. They then look at how much money you owe on each of those cards and add that all together.

The amount owed is divided by the amount available and that's your total balance percentage. You want to keep this percentage low because that reflects well on your credit card. A high percentage is going to look bad and lower your credit score.

The total amount of accounts that you have as well as the types of accounts is going to count towards your score as well. You actually want to have a moderate number of accounts (more than 10) as long as you can keep them all current. You also want to have an assortment of accounts (credit cards, mortgages, car loans, student loans, etc.) this is going to improve your score as well.

Finally, the number of inquiries that you have will affect your score. You want to cut down on the amount of inquiries that you have because every one is a slight ding to your account. What these are is every time that you apply for credit. If you apply they check your credit score and when they check your credit score it goes down a little bit. These inquiries stay on your credit report for some time as well.

That's why you want to apply for credit infrequently and only if you're sure you're going to get it. Getting the credit will help improve your score more than it's going to hurt for the inquiry.

So all in all you want to make sure of a few important things in regards to your credit report:

- Have several different accounts (10 or more)

- Keep all accounts current

- Avoid public records

- Have a variety of types of accounts (loans and credit cards)

- Keep your available balance high

- Keep the balance in use low

- Don't apply for credit unless necessary

- Never apply for credit unless you're sure you'll be approved

- Dispute accounts that aren't correct

- Make payments on any past due accounts and pay off collections

By doing all of these things your credit score will actually increase over time. It will take some time and you're definitely going to need to work at it but you'll be able to bring your credit score back up. Once you're able to bring your score back up you'll find it even easier to get out of debt and you'll start saving better as well.

The reason your credit score is going to affect this is because your credit score actually has a lot to do with you getting approved for everything from credit cards to car loans to housing. It also has to do with the interest rates that you're given. As your score goes up you'll be able to request lower interest rates and that makes it even easier to pay off debts and stay out of debt in the long run. Staying out of debt means you have more money to put away towards your savings. So it's really a win all the way around.

Chapter 6: Ways You Never Knew You Could Raise Your Score

You can actually ask credit card companies to get rid of problems on your credit report even if you are actually in the wrong. What you want to do is simply call or write to the credit card company directly. Let them know that you understand you were late on a payment but point out your history and show that you have not been late in the past and you made a one-time mistake. (If you have been late frequently they probably won't work with you as much.).

Now if you have never made this mistake before or if you have rarely done it the credit card company may be willing to wave a late payment. This would mean that they take the late payment remark from your history and you may not even have to pay a fine. But by taking off the mark on your history they are improving your credit score. That one little late payment can be a big problem and it can result in your score taking a big hit. If it gets removed you no longer have to worry about it and your credit score could go up quite a bit.

Keeping old accounts open is another important way that you can improve your credit score. The oldest accounts that you have are actually improving your credit, whether they are positive or negative. What this means is you could have a long history of late payments with your oldest account but you're getting more positive marks on your credit from that account being so old than you are negative marks for the late payments. You don't ever want to close your oldest account unless you have no way around it. This account is doing great things for you.

Now if you have multiple accounts that are very close to the same age and one has a lot of negative marks you can close it. What you don't want to do is close the only account you have that's older than two years. (Of course, the older the account is the better it is for you.) Only close this account if there's an important reason for it or if you have another account that is very close to the same age and is giving you the same benefits when it comes to account history.

All those 'free quote' websites are actually hurting your credit score as well. You need to make sure that you are not signing up for a lot of those quotes. Even when you're searching for something like car insurance or health insurance you need to be careful. Free quotes may sound great but how do you think they're able to give you that quote? They need to know a little more about you in order to give you something that they can guarantee and that means they run your credit history and check out your credit score. That helps them to know whether you'll pay your bills or not and that affects your quote.

Pay your balance more than once a month. A lot of people use their credit cards for everything. That's either because it's easier to use instead of having to carry around a lot of cash, or because you just want to keep raking in rewards points that you can use for other things. Those are perfectly good reasons and if you're paying off the card every month you're not getting late charges or anything like that which is a benefit to you. On the other hand, you could be hurting your credit utilization rate.

Now you may be thinking, I pay it off every month so how could I be hurting my credit score? Well, when your bank or credit union sends you a bill they are telling you how much money you owe. That amount is also being sent to the credit reporting agency, which uses it to calculate your credit utilization rate. If your balance is $500 and you owe $500 then your utilization rate is 100% and that's going to look really bad on your credit report. It's going to lower your score by quite a bit.

What you want to do is make more than one payment per month. If your balance at the end of the month is lower than the limit then you're going to have a better utilization rate. The lower the rate you have the better it's going to look on your score, so make sure that you're paying as much as you can for each of your payments. That way, no matter when your credit card company sends in the balance owed, you won't get a big hit on your credit report and you'll be able to keep your score higher, where you want it to be.

Before You Go

Thank you again for downloading this book!

I hope this book was able to help you to start saving money, pay off your debt and improve your credit.

Finally, if you enjoyed this book, then I'd like to ask you for a favor, would you be kind enough to leave a review for this book on Amazon? It'd be greatly appreciated!

http://www.amazon.com/review/create-review?ie=UTF&&asin=B00ZVE2G8E

Thank you and good luck!

Check Out My Other Books

Below you'll find one of my other popular books that are popular on Amazon and Kindle as well.

A #1 Amazon Bestseller. Earn a Great Living by Writing a Popular Blog!

How To Start A Profitable Blog: A Guide To Create Content That Rocks, Build Traffic, And Turn Your Blogging Passion Into Profit contains valuable information on how to make money from blogs, build your passive income, and experience financial freedom.

Grab your copy today, for a low price of ONLY, $0.99. Read on your PC, Mac, Smartphone, Tablet, or Kindle Device- Download Your Copy Today! Read This Book FREE on Kindle Unlimited.

http://www.amazon.com/How-Blog-Profit-Step---Step-ebook/dp/B00ZVE2G8E

www.ingramcontent.com/pod-product-compliance
Lightning Source LLC
Chambersburg PA
CBHW070758180526
45168CB00004B/1671